Awesome Addition MAZES

Gabriele Tafuni

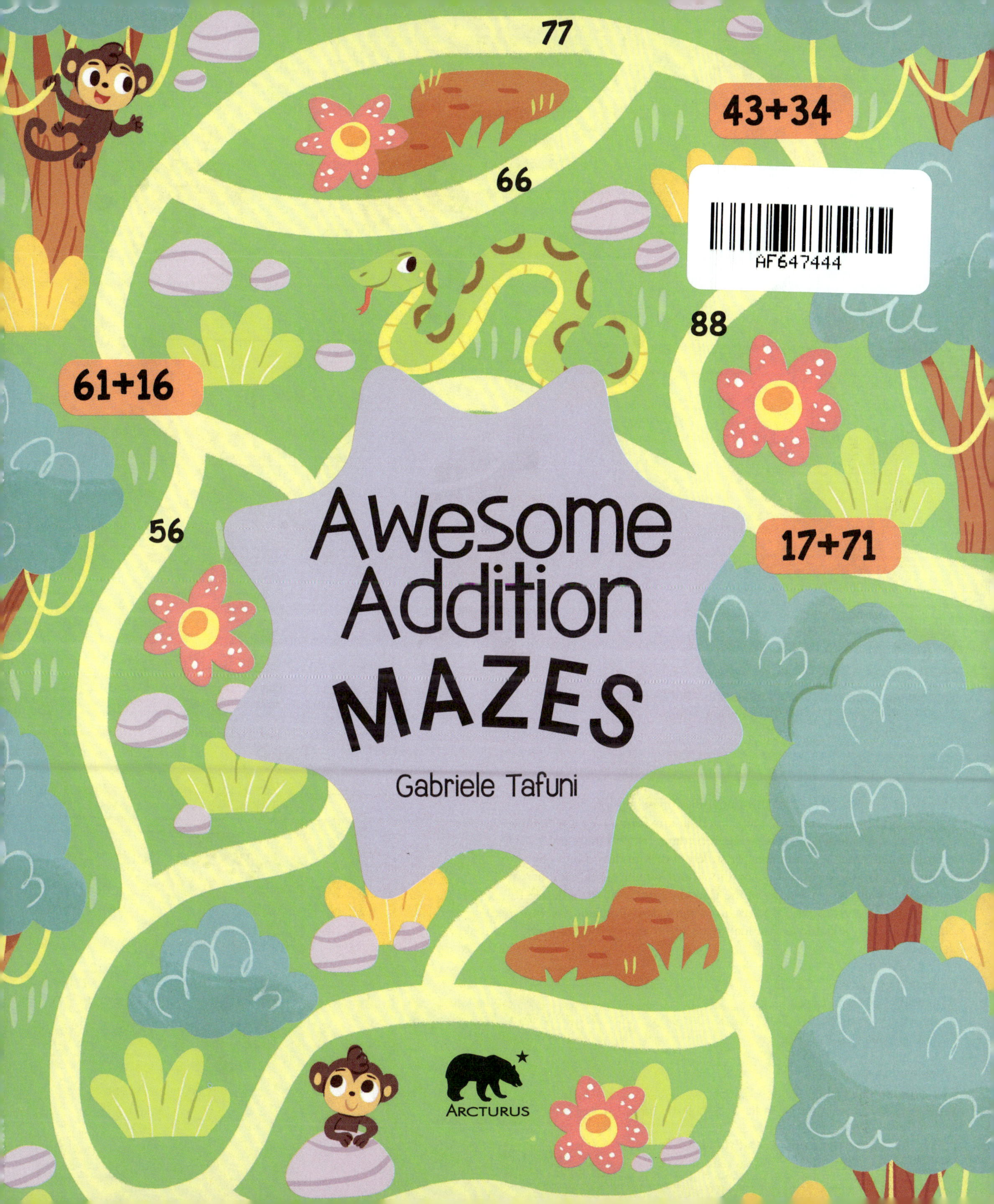

ARCTURUS

ARCTURUS

This edition published in 2020 by Arcturus Publishing Limited
26/27 Bickels Yard, 151–153 Bermondsey Street,
London SE1 3HA

Illustrated by Gabriele Tafuni
Written by Catherine Casey
Designed by Trudi Webb
Edited by Sebastian Rydberg

ISBN: 978-93-5954-894-4
This reprint edition: July, 2025
Published and Distributed in India by Scholastic India Pvt. Ltd.

Printed in India at Acme Print O Pac. Pvt.Ltd. Noida

How to Use This Book

Welcome to the "funtastic" world of awesome addition mazes! This activity book is full of exciting scenes to help you learn and become confident with the basics of addition.

Locate the start of each maze, and read the instructions to help you solve it.

Some topics come with a Top Tip to help you on the way.

Solve each calculation, and then choose the correct path to reach the end.

After you have completed the maze, check that you followed the correct route, by turning to pages 30-32.

Number bonds

Number bonds are pairs of numbers that make up a given number. These are some of the number bonds to 10 and 20.

10 Bonds	20 Bonds
1+9	1+19
2+8	2+18
3+7	3+17
4+6	4+16
5+5	5+15

Totals to 10

Can you guide the girl through the obstacle course to the finish line? Follow the problems that add up to 10.

Finish
5+4
5+2
8+2
6+4
3+7
3+8

Adding

Help the boy speed down the mountain to his ski lodge. Solve the calculations and take the route with the correct answers.

5+3
8+3
11
3+9
11
7
8
10
12
1+4
Finish
3
5

Doubles

Can the diver swim through the fish and coral to the shipwreck? Work out the doubles and follow the correct answers.

Top Tip

A double is where two numbers that are the same are added together.
Double 3 = 3 + 3

Number bonds to 10

Help the children to find their way out of the maze.
Follow the calculations that add up to 10.

Top Tip

Remember that number bonds to 10 can be added in two ways:

3 + 7 = 10

7 + 3 = 10

8+12
8+9
1+19
16+3
15+7
12+8
4+16
11+9
Finish

Totals to 20

Canoe down the river to the campsite.
Follow the calculations that add up to 20.

Numbers to 20

Help the rock climber choose the next handhold by solving the calculations and following the correct answers.

Finish
19
4+15
20
7+11
18
17
5+14
18
19
14
13
2+12

Adding units to two-digit numbers

Direct the builder to the truck. Solve the problems and follow the path with the correct answers.

Finish
65
68
65+3
Top Tip
Start with the bigger number and count on.
48
46
44+4
38
32+6
37
47
45+2
57
58
46
54+4

Adding 10

Guide the boy through the waves to the beach. Solve the calculations and follow the path with the correct answers.

5+10
7+10
17
19
8+10
15
5
18
18
Top Tip
After adding a 10, the units always stay the same.
2+10
12
13
1+10
1
11
14
4+10
4
Finish

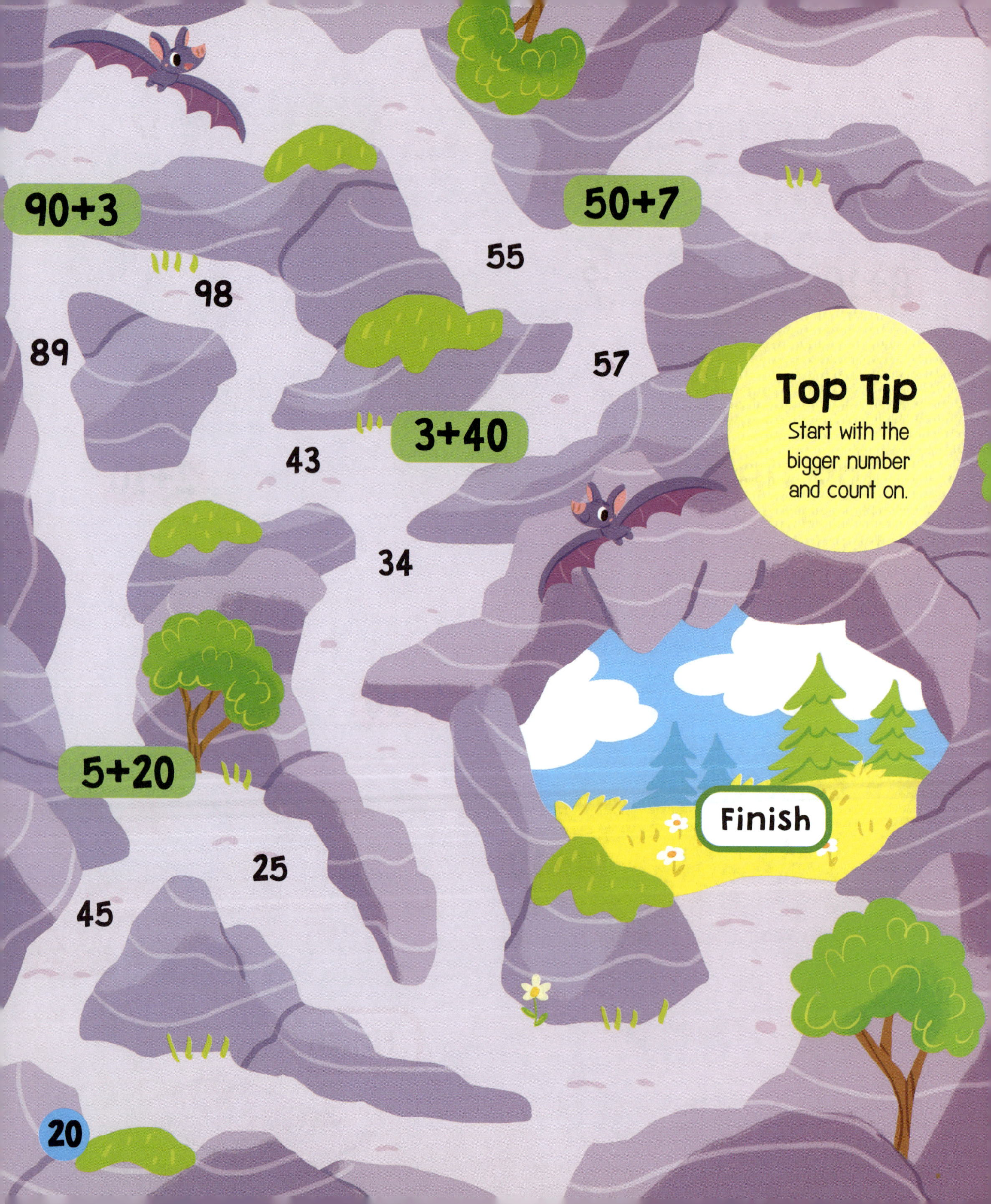

Top Tip

Start with the bigger number and count on.

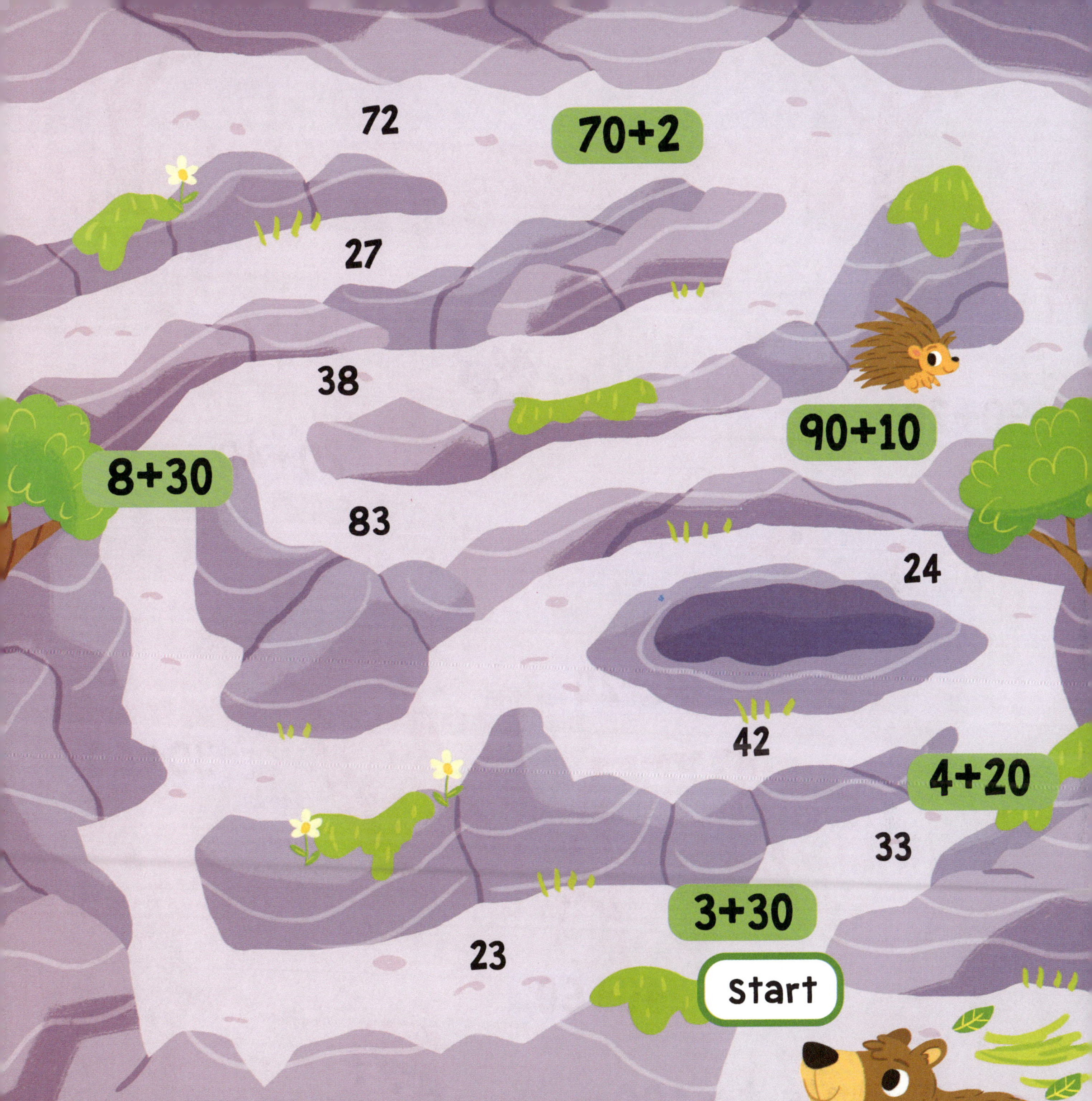

Adding multiples of 10

The bear has just woken up. Lead him out of his cave into the open air. Solve the calculations and follow the path with the correct answer.

Totals to 100

Lead the girl through the park to the skate ramp. Follow the calculations that have a total of 100.

Top Tip

Use your number bonds and place value knowledge to help you, remember

$4 + 6 = 10$ so

$40 + 60 = 100$

Adding 10 to two-digit numbers

Help the alien make her way back to the spaceship. Solve the addition problems and follow the path with the correct answers.

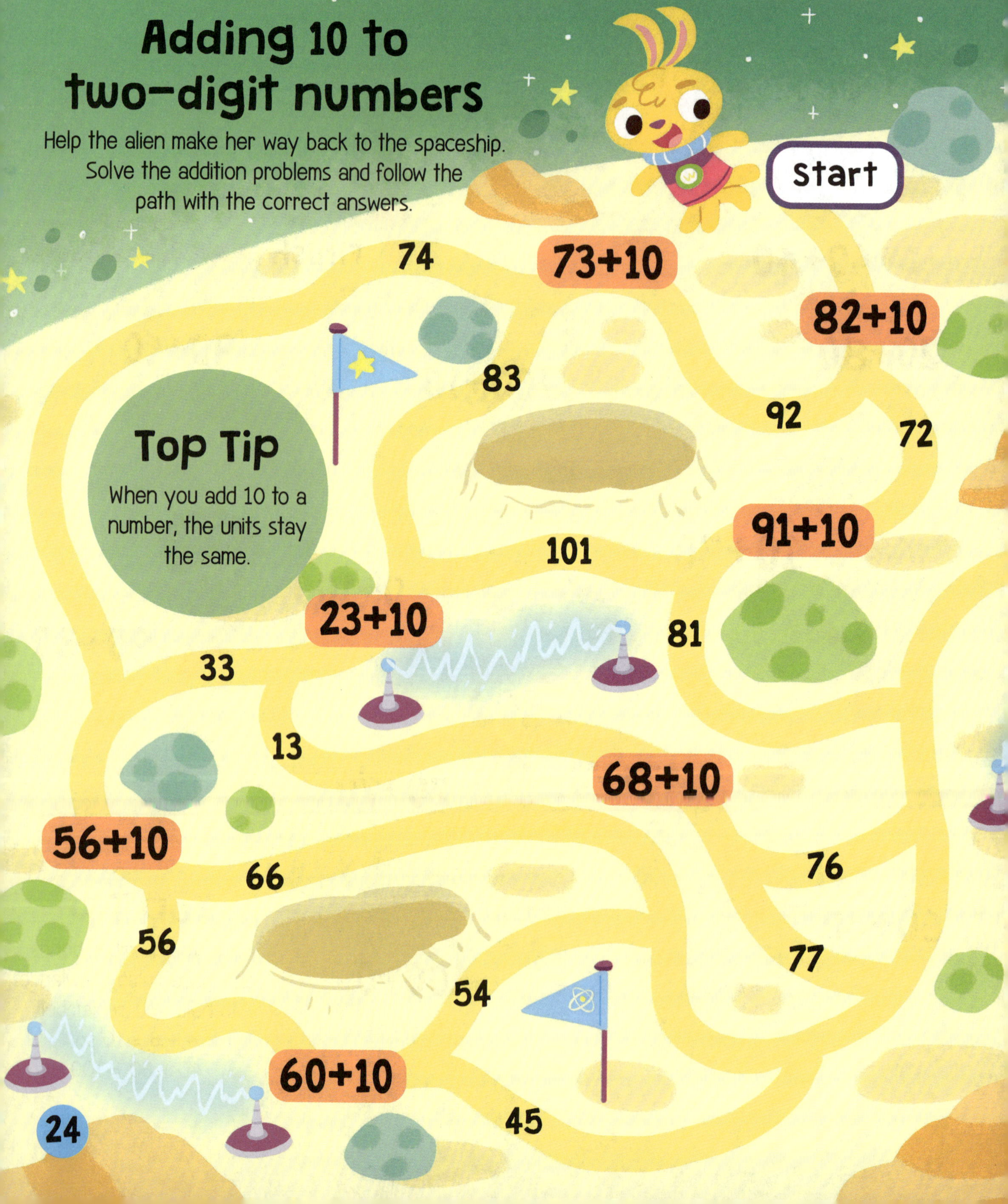

Top Tip

When you add 10 to a number, the units stay the same.

45+10
46
55
27+10
37
37
38
48
38+10
Finish
74
65
12+10
91
22
23
64+10
71
81+10

Adding two-digit numbers

Help the ghost make her way back to the house she should be haunting! Solve the calculations and follow the correct answers.

Top Tip

Add the units first, then the tens.

77
43+34
66
88
61+16
77
78
56
17+71
Finish
83
61+32
93
39
27+12
93

More adding two-digit numbers

Swing through the jungle with the explorer, to the jungle hut. Solve the calculations and follow the correct answers.

ANSWERS

4–5 Totals to 10

6–7 Adding

8–9 Doubles

10–11 Number bonds to 10

12–13 Totals to 20

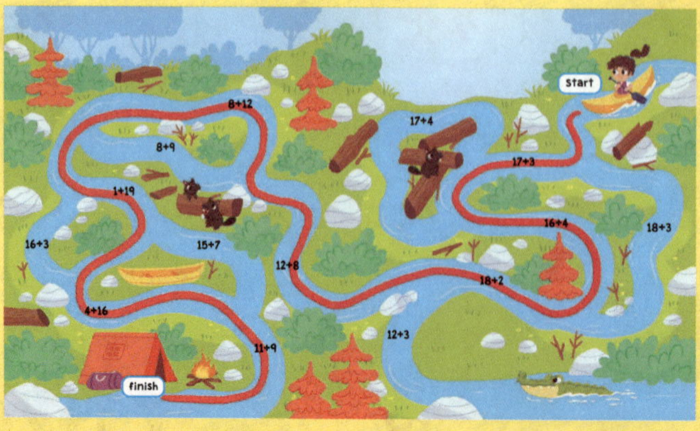

14–15 Numbers to 20

16–17 Adding units to two-digit numbers

18–19 Adding 10

20–21 Adding multiples of 10

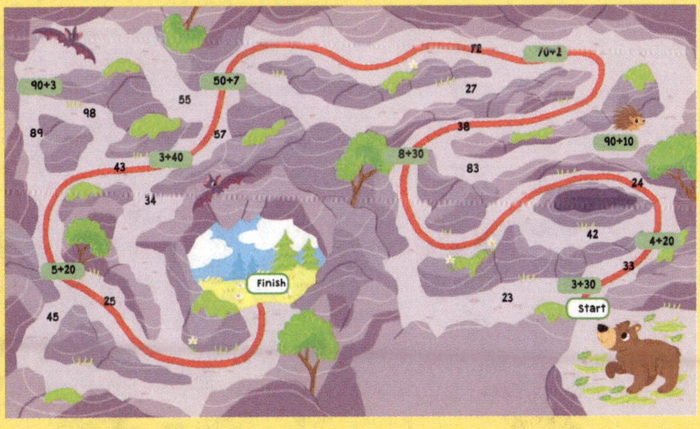

22–23 Totals to 100

24–25 Adding 10 to two-digit numbers

26–27 Adding two-digit numbers

28–29 More adding two-digit numbers